Frederik Fischbach

Lace Album

A series of twenty-six plates of designs for lace

Frederik Fischbach

Lace Album
A series of twenty-six plates of designs for lace

ISBN/EAN: 9783742866578

Manufactured in Europe, USA, Canada, Australia, Japa

Cover: Foto ©Andreas Hilbeck / pixelio.de

Manufactured and distributed by brebook publishing software
(www.brebook.com)

Frederik Fischbach

Lace Album

LACE ALBUM:

A SERIES OF

TWENTY-SIX PLATES

OF

DESIGNS FOR LACE.

BY

FREDERICK FISCHBACH,

Director of the Art Industrial School, St. Gall, Switzerland.

PRIVATELY PRINTED FOR THE AUTHOR.

1878.

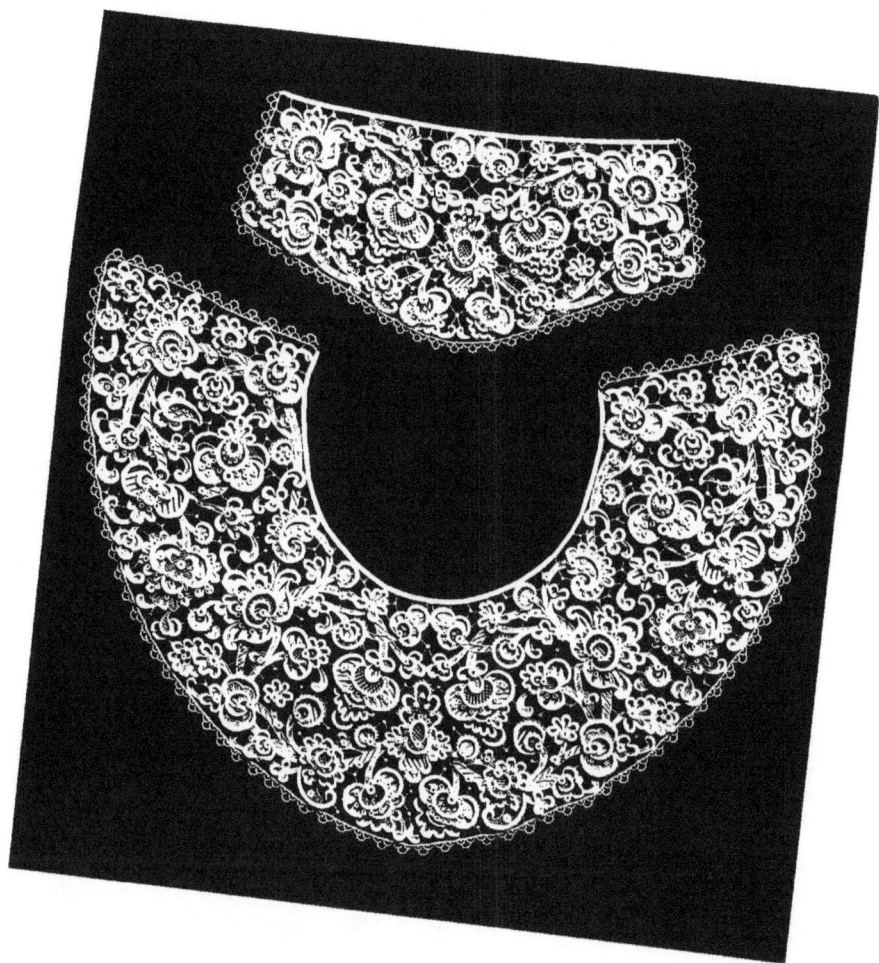

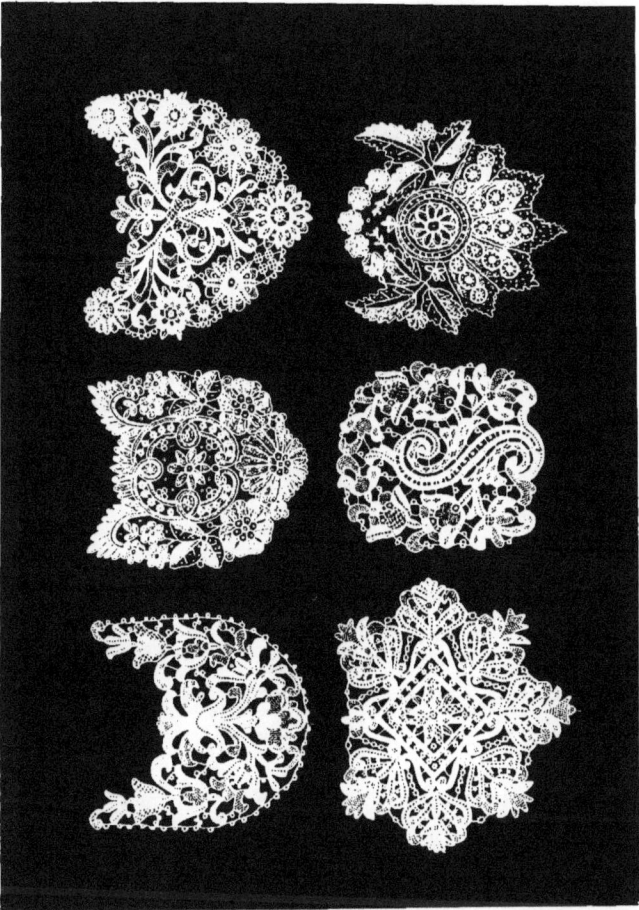

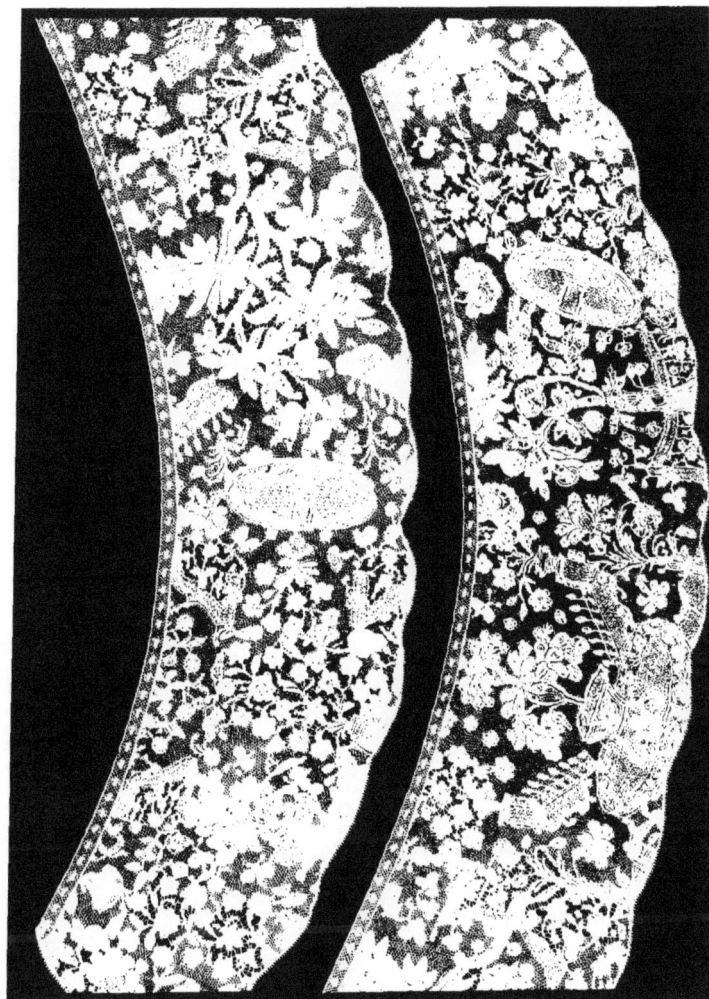

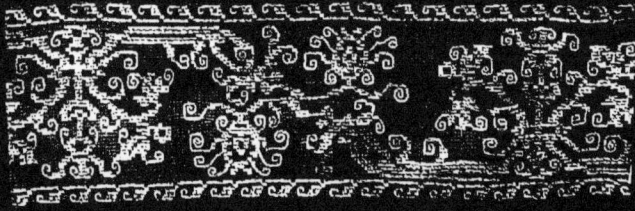

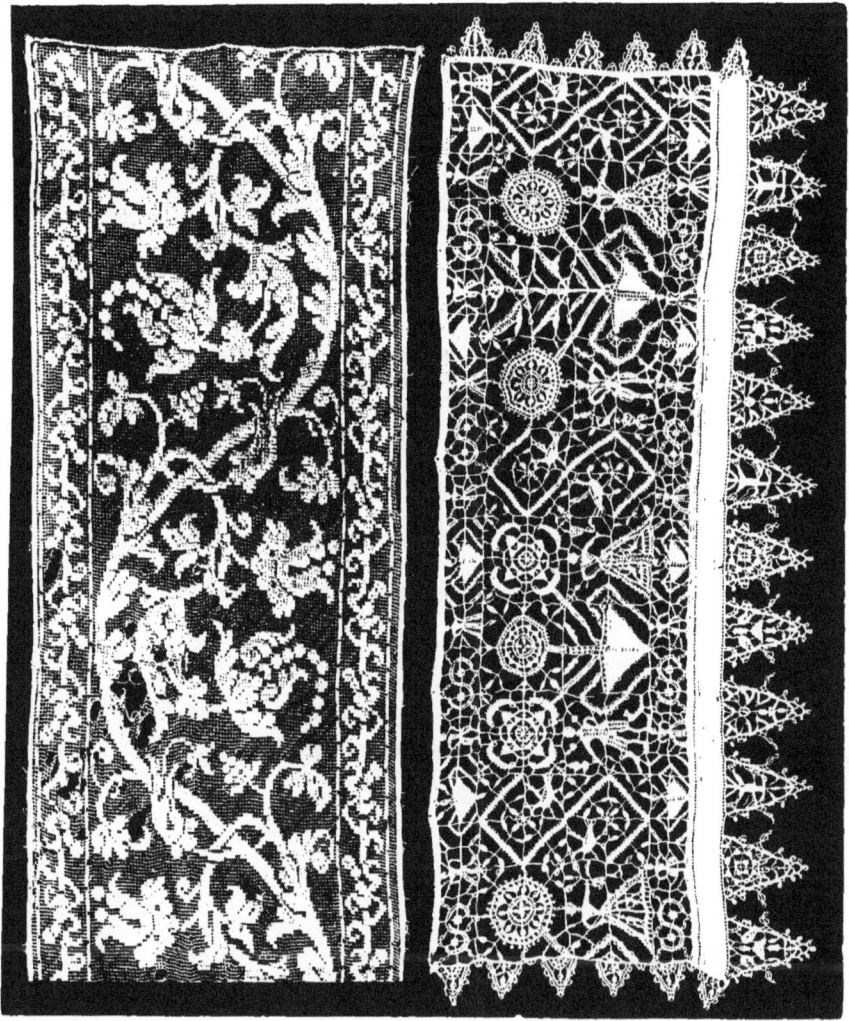

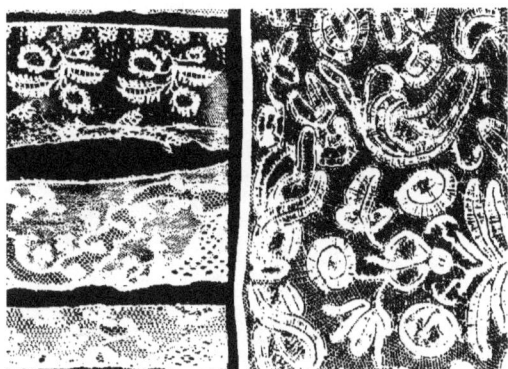

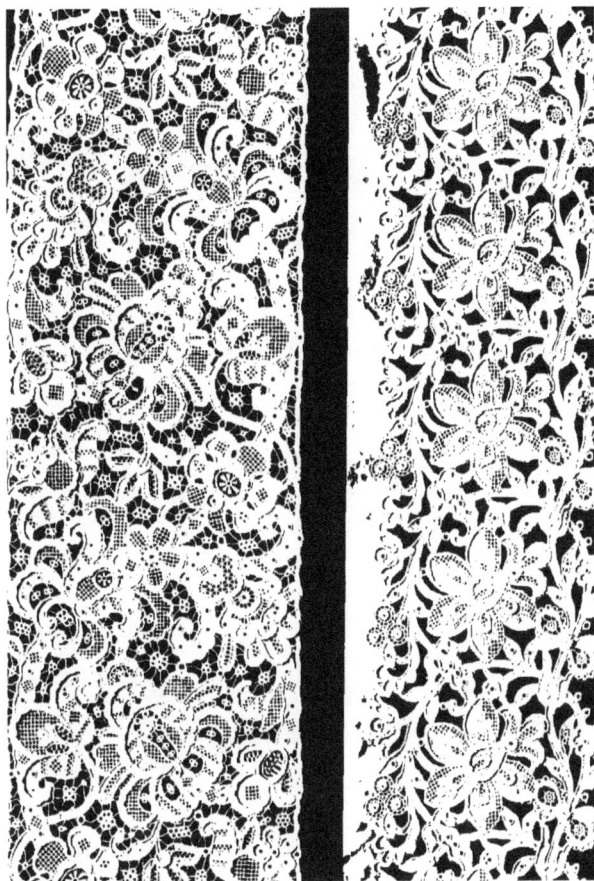

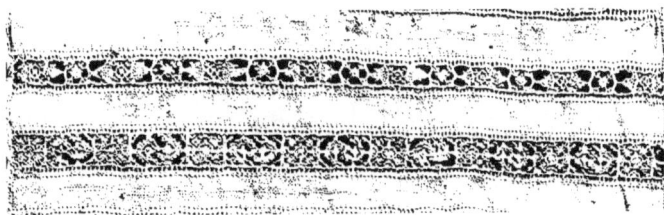